I0399727

little bones in red clay

Al;so by Helga Jermy and published by Ginninderra Press
Firebird Baltic Blue

Helga Jermy

little bones in red clay

GP

I pay my deep respects to the custodians and storytellers of this land we call lutruwita/Tasmania, their elders past, present and future.

For my family. Because you are everything.

little bones in red clay
ISBN 978 1 76109 406 4

Cover: Kitsune Creative Co

First published 2022 by
GINNINDERRA PRESS
PO Box 3461 Port Adelaide 5015
www.ginninderrapress.com.au

Contents

Preface

These poems are an unearthing: a small and personal quest to discover why we pursue the things we do – why we migrate, why art matters, how political dialogue sparks our veins, how love of landscape makes us tread carefully but awkwardly.

Living here in lutruwita/Tasmania, gently, in the slow hiss of our deflating planet, I look for cause and effect, truth and fable. We are just little bones in air or clay, but how we spin and swoon and rebel in the light.

a baby wren
a kookaburra
one inside the other

Beginnings

at the beginning of things
things had already begun.

so many circulations of sail and flight, before
        a fat black night
        passes through
        consuming the clouds
        on its way with us to outer margins.

here in the 35,000 feet of suspension
        in the swell of uplift
in the bones and blood and breath
        so much trust in steel joints   air pockets
plastic wrapped water

flight hours are illusion
dizzy with virtual time
dusty covers of stanzas
and engineered dis-ease.

landed like a leaf
        we're windswept like so many others.
                blown to shore from sky.

Sometimes memory is an awkward stranger

a plane about to land, the sky
tosses us into bright blue outcrop
        strung with cirrus
        a strange red earth beneath us,
        scarred, fraught, intruded
        wisped with flower and teatree,
        whipped twist of invasive winds.

what made me pack
a half-lived life into crates
with sundry choice of obsessions
bricolage of human foils and baggage
        the size of one point two containers?

what made us
fight interior ministries
with proof of value in ticks and loopholes
to join the young and free
when we acknowledge the old and ancestral?

sometimes memory
is an awkward stranger,
slick with invention.

I mean only to be still
to tread softly the bracken and bone
the hop and leaf, the gull and shell, all the salt
and light and scented gum,
the snakes that bite, the bumbling bee
who predated my fumble and dawn.

but still, I am alien footprints on sand.
English viridian on ochre –
how our colours travel with us.
and blind us.

        here, the sun knows our small mercies.
        but abstracted still
                we are unresolved.

This walk, this wildness

this path we're on,
    this wild imagining
    wet and worn,
        weary even

in the space between branches
    strange weather
    advancing   and we're held here
        in its caprice

shed snakeskin on lichen
little fungi pops
amongst the gum shoots
fire-stain   flood-mould
litter lurking   fallen nest
boot-tread and bone-crunch
    all the burrowed wombats
    waiting for the bark-grey shield of night

sanctuary here, and silence
gold leaf without the hammering
a touch of rust

alpine yellow gum and
beaked needlebush at Cradle
in cloud today
    dreaming of rain

little bones in red clay
birdsong pressed into bark-vellum
all the notes in feathered filiform
          beneath this   link and lament
     all root and filament   holding on

brief sunlight
     catches in a web

          she-oak looks up
          contemplates
          the glass ceiling
     in all its ragged exuberance

     mauve cloud sky
     shaking its silver branches
     hiker-breath and ghost-hair
     all psalm thoughts   then gone

some bent architecture is bowing to the void
     withered branch, pith and trunk
     a solitary kangaroo paw sent forward
     in search of life.

this walk, this wildness –
          a wattlebird frees its song into the flow

Flood proof

the flood passes me by
in a grunge run down the valley
drenched bandit
gathering its flotsam
sunlit starlit litter

the foreshore is a velodrome to lost particles

    we are told not to touch
    the sea foam
    so fizzy
    its bubbling froth
    is pure sewage

the tide creeps back in shock and shame
bloodline stuck in a rip has had a gut full

downdrift pitches to a silver floating tone
    shifting the microplastics

bloated cattle carcass
exclaims its grief in the shallows
twitched mast of a dinghy
pokes its tongue out
of splintered waters

split hank
of fisherman's rope lies rotting with fish heads
frayed nerves exposed
a hole gapes in the bridge's flank
containers dropped like space junk
on rolling bearings

the foreshore has heard this all before

sand bags are fat and heavy
the river bank has gobbled the crops and buried the dead

Firewatch

there is a scarlet wash dripping
                                        with burnt milk grey
in the space between sky and distant tree blaze.

we watch an approaching single chopper with all
the water
        it can muster head for the burnished war front
spotlit with stray embers.
                calls for an early response have been
lost in spin chatter on drip feed.
                trickle me down. trickle me
a shower in the firmament safe from budgetary analysis.

the brambles have lushed and retreated.
                        an orchard blushes
in the potent signature of alarm.

                a ringtail wakes early to
check on the foliage.
        hurries her way back in that cumbrous gait
                to her scratchy home in the garage roof space.

        we have sprayed and sprayed with a hose.

we are not in control but like to think we are. we wait
for updates and reinforcements.   we won't sleep at all.

aftermath is a passing newsfeed.
                apparently, the pollies
might as well be the bird kind.
                we have no claims to fill, luckily.
there will be crowdfunds for others.

driving past the ghost pines in the reduced sentence
of morning, the recomposed air
        has turned hound grey and wheezy.
we pass an indignation of blistered gums
                        scribbling the fog plumes
with newly charcoaled slogans.
                scrub ash just kilometres away
from our supposed refinements.
                there are charred remains

where usually there is roadkill.   all roads leading to new
definitions of death by disaster.   a tragicide.

by the gate I leave you chopped salad and a water bath.
I know you are a pest, little one
        you folivore, coriander thief with
predatory tastes for anything netted and fenced.
        but I am/we are
bigger pest/s in the scheme of grub-greed and enclosures.

                        the sky
has shrugged off its unfamiliar reasons and plunged
into decorous afternoon rose.
        how easy it is to drive through the valley now.
its paths crossing the paths.
                a smell of exigency briefly forgotten.

Immature fruit

wren's nest
silk strung to mulberry
feathered bones below.

red earth spiced
with pepper berry
and banksia needles.
my hands dig digging
jumping ants biting back.
by my side, a bloodied
pademelon joey
who couldn't be saved
from the wheels of a car.
limbs of cherry
a slow contortion above us
stretching out and on
overhanging
this little ceremony
with immature fruit.

winding path
a tiger snake slithers
to shade.

Weathered

perhaps we should give up chasing down the paragraphs
as they newsfeed until stop full.
it is sand snow sculpted this page,

defies its dimensions,
but I prefer it to the blue-light screen, isobarred.
outside the rain says stay in

but you know you never listened before.
perhaps in a kilometre or two, the stones beneath the creek
are telling stories of the dry.

the weather is such a dominatrix.
yesterday we locked the windows from fire haze,
lavender sky and stained moon.

it is snowing in New York and we all have to freeze in it.
I lost my thermostat in the Cumbrian floods.
there is a high over New Delhi.

if only it wasn't summer it would be winter but
here there is no place for the faint-hearted. skin
wrinkles, burns and chaffs before its shedding.

perhaps I'll wear perhaps I won't.
oh, for a fall streak cloud to add to the tension –
the drifting cirrus uncinus is such a tease.

Weeds

with casual disregard, attuned,
as we are, to our own aesthetics,
I have tossed these
blue flowered speedwell
from the comfort of warm dirt
into nothing.   again, and again,
and again, their tiny, but abundant growth,
refuses to give way
to my will for control.
azaleas don't like it here.   nasturtiums
are nibbled by night creatures.   zinnias
curl up to die.
in morning glow, there is that small,
persistent green again;
shoots that speed well.   weed, weed,
where is your pride?   stretching into light,
dancing with bees,
lying with dandelions.
today I see your many petalled joy and free myself
from invasive thinking,
unfurl in daisy white and pastel.
the path is my path,
but the moss does not know it.
what are foxgloves good for?
perhaps ask your ageing heart.

Turning of the fagus

ancient/ thin twisted
limbs/ clasp
of roots where the
quoll hides/

tanglefoot hold
with lyric lines
of persistence
& memory
weft through shallow
earth/ round dolerite/
by creeks/ along cold
mountains/ nests/ burrows/
paths & button grass
writing/ shaping a story
in a cellular
Gondwanaland language

as I stand mute/
over wombat &
tiger snake track/
autumn colours turn
butter/ russet/ red/
leaves shed gold
on my feet/
I am mutant in the mix/
grounded
over the whirl of time/
to sounds of breeze/
rain/ whispering veins/
shed bark/ leaf flow/
bird call & breath

Epicurious

such things that diets are made of: termites
from the woodpile inside the wren, the egg inside the hen
that is now inside of me, the scraps the pig eat, your pork
your bacon, the termite mound full of bark and whispered
ghosts, the bug inside the apple inside the goat inside
the cheese inside the pie on your plate,
the festering alien inside the guts inside the lies
inside the president, the buried tree inside the coal
inside the bank accounts inside the hidden assets,
the gas inside the polymer inside the fish
inside the batter inside the fryer, the bird
inside the chimney inside the smoke inside the sky.

coffee at the beach
watching the seagulls squabble
a haiku walks by

Beach

Beach of cool forgotten limpets
Beach of bottle and bling and quartz lush
Beach of drone shot pixels
Beach of rippled moonthroat full of lumber
Beach of claw and threat and shellscar
Beach of corking cotton, washed up ball and anchor
Beach of blunderstress and sharkblood
Beach of groyne in shifting tidal
Beach of steel wreck fringe with ghostheart
Beach of drift-bled oil spill
Beach of single use styrofoam havoc
Beach of rust on an android fossil
Beach of dead fish wrapped in plastic
Beach of storm and drunken strobe light
Beach of human-handed carbon
Beach of anthropo scene drowning drowning

Monofilament is best

you are sharp as a cuttlefish blade,
white as its textured sheaf,
the brine is shuffling round your ankles
playing with your line
as I leave your retort to the crusted barnacles and silent seal skull.

looking back, I watch as you flick the line,
flick again, find some
rhythm in the pulse of the wavering tide.
        the sky is a gunmetal grey,
tight as a drumhead before the cadence of a marching
                band beats its groove and meter.

you are taut, precise.
you say the fish like rain, stand your sandy ground,
defy the wind. it is three days now
        since you spilt that mortal ash from the tinnie.
        you hit the line
on the skin of water, defy its thievery.

there is shivering canine loyalty at your heel.
his whine implores the breathing air
and the wheezing mist, sings to your lost horizons.
        there is death bait in your bucket,
a pull of expectations, no stomach for guts,
                a line of glass and carbon.

All the bar-tailed godwits paddling in a flock

little spindled legs cooling in the breach
before take-off with zoom racket
into the demi blue of skyscape.
they're such gang stirrers
and it bothers me that the sky rips like that
in the squawk of a flock
so I'm back in my book. briefly.
spindly legs below wings that can navigate
the globe are distracting.
I have invited their beak flutes to picnic.
they're muttering some stem sentence,
something about cabin fever.
the moonrise is not yet nostalgia
before I notice that the tide has swallowed my Camus.
and it seems kind of appropriate in this age
of all show and Kardashian.

Ocean

the man at the end
of the bay thinks he owns
this beach, its tides and temper
fish flesh & flora.

the man in a dune drift
with rights
in rolled up chinos
& tatty straw boater.

here on damp shore
ask the ocean though.
littoral
larking

about in salt lick
tossing the night's
gifted urchins
starfish sailfin & glass.

the ocean's slick
seal skin
peeling at the edges
in a crash

of spume & algal bloom
white ribboned
noisy as rip & rupture
holding its secrets

in cosmogenic rust
& stipe blade weed
hiding its bone relics
its ship shapes

its lost living morsels
its skulls & maps.
here are its own rights
& lefts.

6 equal pieces

two gulls squawk and defecate
on the head of a penguin statue.
here in the state's north-west it
is just an idle gesture like tide
pounding marbles on beach walls.
the bay is a bad act of geometry.

we can only cartwheel when the
tide is out two times daily lunar
calculations on flat mud sand.
a thousand shells spiralling despite
a lack of golden principle. one greedy
tern empties the cup of a whelk.

the bus glides through twice a day.
baristas stare out to horizons whilst
frothing hearts on flat whites.
the wind smashed boat shed
has become a kind of rhomboid
minus its sharply accurate degrees.

on the gradient someone points
a telescope to far ambitions.
infinity in figure of eight circles
plays light tricks on the headland
and it could just be illusion but it
could relatively be a ray theory.

a couple seeking clear parameters
in the angler's cove overestimate
some blue blasted expressive need.
on the jetty flathead gape in ab-
sense of sea. bucket list adding and
subtracting something more solid.

perhaps there are solutions but
the sun is incandescent white today
the sky an ivory white, the sails
hypotenuse against white flotillas,
the hulls riding perturbations that
propagate through waves of water.

Boat Harbour

I'm told that the rock is igneous, volcanic,
precambrian. it is also fossilised motion,
twists, gnarls and punched fist.
it is dancing pools of fire and ice, wild colourisation
in flamenco skirts, rivers rolling molten
through honeycomb, caverns and capers and chaos.
we sit here west of the wind, our ears and noses burning
in the relentless eye of the sun.
the sand is fine sifted. small granulations of time.
beneath us there are rumbles in the plasma.
the tides have reached their morning horizons
and are about to change direction.
the gull with a broken leg scores a fish.
the gull with its dominant squabble and squawk
is all ancestral feather and bone.
the gull with crumbs is helicopter parenting.
they don't care at all how I plan to vote on Saturday.

Electrochromic

sea smoke near Stanley is a conjuror's fog,
a little teasing dance across the sandbar
of my cloudy notions.
incoming sails are no more than albatross wings
scattering fine crystals, a dewy kind of coastal sentiment
when I'm only looking for a break in the weather.
two kids on the beach are alarmingly translucent:
one pink puffer coat a veil
of juvenile floss in the breakers;
one brine soaked yellow flicked
like a stroke from a squirrel haired brush.
when I call them back, the albatross caw
echoes their screeching in the fallen cloud
of afternoon, little footprints dancing back
through fine granite and airborne salt.
they're not put off at all by the swoop of birds
or the wet face slap of vapour
or the yappy call to leave. each cup of hands
is a bowl of watery shadows and beams, tricks of light
pretending to be fish. we eat hot chips,
our breath beneath the lava plug of the Nut
with silver scales. as we drive away, a fogbow smudges
its colour; another mocking in the smart glass of car wings.

Skua's song

the sky weaves blue a skua's sung strand.
glacial blur an iceberg calf's reflection.
from gull's eye into lakes under ice
where is the heartbeat the breath the cry?
time's loose tongue against our genome lips?
how can music be metered in our chaos?
here where the ice hurts.
there where blink and albatross.
somewhere where fish fly low composing symposia.
so many press and beep and softkey calls
forgotten but for interstellar memory.
still the sky weaves its iterations.
each snow pile winged with droplets.
each droplet tomorrow's freeze.
sky clouds in blue weaving a song for gull
and ice melt, an ocean's lift and downflow.

Swimming above the belly of the earth

Suppose I was a wave and the gulls' feet
sought only to rest on my skin,
this skin that breaks at every moment
only to resurface with new tone and texture.
Suppose the undertow cared not one jot for foam
and oil, hoping to toss its loitering
mass of non-consumables through the exit of my mouth.
All my senses would be alive
with the tug of moon and tide, swimming above
the deep belly of the earth's iron core.
Suppose this; that the juts of quartz feel fresh
in my spit and spray, and, as I lay still,
exhausted, they mirror in the calm
as mortals do before they die.
I would wash into the rhythm of sand,
embrace the fluid and unfathomable,
the air with its turbulence and hum.
Suppose these movements, wild and lithe,
have moods that change when sleepless.
Or they don't sleep at all but wander dreamless
in vast shifting paradigms,
absorbing time with salt and lost cargo.

beneath the colour purple
red and blue pixels
in perfect unity

Red mountain

After Jason Cordero's *The Day of the Mountain*

the mountain has been rendered red
in a bloodshot light.   I am happy to be guided
by the painterly.   give me also
shade in complementary colours,
the blazing cradle cap a worrying concept
despite the startle reflex setting into warmth.
I have walked the perimeters in dry ochre
I have climbed the stairs that others built
to steer me from free expression.
there is a calling here, a feeling of someone
else's home. an artist and his iridescent
glass perhaps has met them. a snake
avoids us, on a real walk earlier,
seeking better morsels and pure water of lake.
it has a way of sensing mainly movement, the blinding
red conceptual.
the trees are stark cut and arrow.
the water drunk on crimson.   I'm drawn into that red
like the lost stranger that I am.   all for
another way of seeing
with the road ahead in flame.

Landscape with illusion

Oh, the glorious art of Dorrit Black

Dorrit changed the colour of it; sunlit yellow
where some concept of green should be
in the overhead canopy.
                              the road
has turned voluptuous orange; all smooth deception,
as it should be, in a dream or on a canvas.

too much reality clouds the senses.

lush columns of ochre in my garden –
bright day and shadow browns.
a brush of hip on a far tree,
a milky breast consuming
leaves. in the foothills a sketch of thighs
rolling in the splendid grass.

on the beach, Dorrit dances
and all the gulls are flying sails.
light billows then retracts with smooth shading.
a face appears and it is an invitation
to wander in closer.

                    for that is what we do in landscapes –
round the corner, dissolve in air, lose the bias edge.
the beach here is washed with life, dissolving into ocean,
the morning tide fat with wanting.

Softly the sand

Thoughts after the Glover exhibition, Launceston

softly the sand sifts through its colours in rain.
who can tell me what hour it is here
in the bent light of fading summer?

        softly the sand, I feel its perforations of granite,
its powdered sea and sound shell.
emerald afterthoughts, wet sun on everything,
a paradiddle instrumental as tern song.
thoughts along the dream day
        turn to currawongs on birch panel,
        to acrylic roads of separation,
        to the back land where red loams
a potato patch, farmers just as rooted.
it's all an exhibition or artscape in recovery mode.
        move inland for masonite and fencing.
        trees assemble along the battery line,
        sketch bats against the sun.
foaming in ocean
an idea of abalone in charcoal relief
with stirrings of under-seasoned orange.
tongues tied against mutton fish
iridescent nacre hidden.
        I have walked here. your naked feet
        baked in parallel prints.
the tides don't surprise us any more
though baggy oceans toss us sideways.
sea we see is weed and shanty.
rampant rusted vegetation back burns offside.

we can't go back again.
our lungs can't carbon sift the shifting forest floor,
its remembered bark and skin.
we pitch our canvas against the highlights
as an undertow of chicks
cry out from crèches for snack packs.
sea clans huddle in the silence of magnets
plot an inward rolling of tidal wire.
it is all so familiar the ghosting dusk recomposing
the coast and line breaks singing to the ancient eucalypts.

softly the sand is grinding pink to pink,
an effervescence to feast the salt seekers.
nothing sleeps in the underwhirl.

Dead bull art at MOFO

art fed innards of a bull carcass,
bos taurus necromance on steroids,
in the dismembered gantry,
in the midwinter of our disconnect,
in the midst of makeshift butchery,
in the ink of dead creatures.

Hermann is in town, detractors in the gallery.
meat | blood | fish | blood | fruit | bones | offal | blood / whistle\

all the white-clad troopers arriving like choristers
before an elegy, before a blood-letting, before a nude swim
to disgorge and purify.
\
I have fed \
on meat / on livers \ /
on oxtail /
I have fed /
on the installations of feast nights \
I have fed \
on the deep-fried gristle of chickens in Tokyo /
/ the wild boars of the Baltic \
\ the octopi of deep oceans /
/ the smoked fish of dying harbours \
I have fed \ /
on the brains of other poets /
/ the gall of politicians \
\ the creative juices of artists ///

in these days of blood vowels and blowflies
there are confessions in the delicatessen
confections in the animal farmed imports.

I am not a member of this strange procession
(although in a way we all are).
I am without
the sacrament of blood swallow \
blindfold /
\ blood streaks /
blood dye /
\ blood in my eye /
blood stain \
/ blood curd \\
blood beneath my nails /
in ears \
in fine nasal airways /
\ blood stuck to the insides of a he-womb /
/ in the gory story of us all \\\

I cannot bring myself to bear witness
(as the peppered mask of my plastic
wrapped steak and kidney can attest to).

I cannot paint the floor red with raw testimony,
feel my hair larded with bull fat /
bull oils \
lipids /
dripping \
/ rendered or otherwise. \
\ I cannot be tied with venal waste /
\ cartilage/ jangled nerves \
intestinal tracts /
\ nor be hit around
my precious head with lungs /
and lesser organs\
\
the earth is red as inflammation,
scarred with cuts and crevices,
cooked in charcoal and kerosene, vamped and in mourning.

what happened to his bones, his leather?
whose feet will be shod here and bags be tanned?
who will hide their silversides in bread now?
their minced flesh in panko crumbs?

in a Salamanca bar the talk is of fluorescent light shows
and other palatable diversions.

the beer is vegan barley haemorrhaging
a reproachful hint of gelatin,
the scratchings just another old salted pork.

The poppy pickers

they're bent over in fluoro like poppies soaked in rain,
although their stalks seem much more brittle.
preoccupied, in profile, they're posed like nineteenth
century Millet gleaners searching for spare change.
the years between are a sequence of hard labour, the chain
linked now by cash strapped backpackers. opium picking
has a nice ring about it for future storytelling, though reality
is bruised and scratched in hot red earth with threat of snakes.
it's a slow procession in furrows where once there were white petals,
a few red rogues in the resistant genealogy. keep out.
there is something arresting about being fenced in on the wrong side
with public warnings. keep out. by dusk there are spinal creaks and groans,
and still the bark of orders. wages relate to rates of production.
all rights are wrong in this image, the pastoral more postmodern.

Sudden shower over Ulverstone Bridge

after Hiroshige

as I bend in those lines of sleet, hold the fragile skeleton ....
of shelter above my head, a twig snaps in etched ....
vertical slashes, fish fall in droplets, bounce ....
off the stillness of us into the river´s mouth. ....
from my vantage, I am suspended ....
on the open bridge, agape in night air ....
lost in my colour, headed home before time freezes. ....
all the distant mountains stand weak and horizontal in nocturnal hue ....
a lone fisherman draws in his line, rows for safety, and we are ....
fully sketched, heads down, heads cold, heading off. ....

Farmland Coastal

After Patrick Grieve's Farmland Coastal Series No. 30

sit a while on the hill and you see the farmland fringe
redact itself, abstracting into ocean.

colour fractures the landscape.
you top it with a line of blue, call it sea,
cover it with an endless sky
that washes into light pickle green
and stills the polychrome brilliant reds
of poppy, the stippled olive and cabbage,
the constant flow of export and returns
that wander in and out on the tide
like a farmer's pulse.

a hint on the horizontal promises no escape.
white horses are rushing into shore
or drown in rips beneath daily toil and confusion.
the sun that strikes the glossy film hovers
out of sight, its crystal incision bright as a chandelier.
sheds are stark white naked,
steely toned. viridian made the trip south
but its borders are hard black wired, devoid of hedges
and barbed against all nostalgia.

we heave and axe, and sow and reap,
and splash our colours beneath a weight of air.
breath ignites behind our sailcloth,
inflames red earth. obligations to other species
are scattered where seeds won't grow.
we've stippled it with wheat. allergens are airborne.
tiger snakes won't make it past the cherry shed,
our fingers stained cerise.
there is a snap and crackle behind us in the timber fall.

power cut
the wind has snapped
its branches

Jury duty

we're through voir dire,
with all our faults and limitations,

the evidence before us is a lengthy
brief (an altercation, beer

and bias, a skull's white cupped
frailty cracked against a wall)

and we're just peers peering in on
back stares of discomfort, wondering

if the kids are home from school,
if the paintings reached the gallery,

if last night's Tuscany pork will stretch
to a kind of cassoulet, then graphic

piercings to inattention, cuts
through flesh and bone, seething

words spat with such ferocity
that DNA is found in an eye socket,

knuckles smashed into brick a bloody
signature underwriting one more loss,

and the tight knot in my stomach
is another twisted gristle punch of revenge.

Minor domestic emergencies

on condition of anonymity the glass breaks its silence. little shards all over my dual national allegiances while wondering what to wear for Albo's disco. fast cooking and oven fat catches a flare of my self-doubt and burns the afternoon's silent recriminations. the walls have inched in like inhaled ribs while we wait for another by-election citizen saga but it is a chance to meet and greet a finely opposing minister whilst engaging in cultural necessities such as bidding for misogyny speech tea towels. the canapés are delicious by the way. and the wine is a speech away from fresh highway upgrading while the famous DJ looks for a knob on the deck to turn down the background fuzz. so many hi hugs synchronised air kissing and oh there's Justine. Tony is in town too. carrots not onions this time. all tastes catered for. posters. pop up party palaces. theories attaching social cellular strobe lit junkets to diffused spin and high hopefuls. the climate is a vacillating political compass point. hands in pockets to counter the corporate advertising splurge of those who dare to challenge; he whose face has shone marrow-like in cascades of comic con. this area is full of pumpkins and glass houses. this soil rejects pink eye potatoes but tolerates tall poppies and their beguiling opiate contradictions. we have tin in our bowels, a seam of tough extracted minerals, a stream of door-knocking volunteers well-seasoned to the quick getaway. there is an aggregated churn in the loam. there is a hint of dissension in the state led ranks as we lurch into federally funded devil in the small print deciphering the treachery in minor revolutions. seven more weeks of blitz burgers. Albo has us dancing to flame trees as we stand by her and the room is a cup half full of pinot grigio. there is such reassurance in the sound waves of spun soul. the drive home is a scattering of domestic possums out for a free feed avoiding truck wheels. red-eyed when caught in the headlights. I wish I'd had three hundred bucks for that signed misogyny speech tea towel.   oh, the irony in the washing up.

A poem with needles in it

a woman is arrested
for sitting and knitting in a chair
outside the door of parliament.
an absence of anger
just yarns from a sheep's back
and a chair placed for restraint
and quiet activity.
click of needles click click.
the politics of days.
the clock resists any need to slow down.
click click
the wool tells its story
which is of warmth and giving
of making a future
and of the need to correct tension.
'if we need to protest extinction
why not do it sitting down?'
one knitting woman says
as she smiles at those dressed in red
and resists the orders of those in blue.
so, they arrest a woman for knitting.
the news reports that she is in good spirits.

streak of lightning
echoes echoes
in the barking dog

Coolish

the first frost to whiten the broad
lane of camellias
is sharp as wit, a stark crystallisation,
an inhale of gloss.
I am smacked in the senses
by its bold hoary cheek.

a wren looks startled in her puffed up
wan feather duster. surveying her surrounds
she stays a while then escapes the early morning picket
for a shelter of eaves.

the lane wanders off to wonderland.
the fleeting snow is a white-out, almost.
a tease, of course. a one-day comic marvel.

it's coolish here. the colour of irony.
I want to be a snow angel, feel
ice on my skin, feel a burn of white rime,
feel flaky, feel anything.

we can almost make a snowball.
we can almost freeze the news out, toss ice particles
on fake serenity while the earth reddens.
we skid like drunks.

so cool the crisp footprints,
the bell-sharp sound.
the flowers are startled pink
unaware of their fate.
cryonic, they still strike a perfect pose.
so cool in this age of flood and fire.

Well, it's kind of expected here

white metal door clasp frayed like old dentistry.
godforsaken glitter ball floating beyond its era
   soon to be replaced by industrial chic as in the pool room.
fizz with everything in old tumblers.
I have glossed my expectations with vicissitudes.
cold beer and pizza disarming the veins,
a distant buzz of farm machinery or is it penitential tears
of bikies roaring their glorious.
    by the bar a perplexed tourist
                        who expected devils in the driveway.
by the bar my niece, who thinks she's wandered onto
an abandoned film set.
by the bar an old dog's territorial ceremonies.
the night too spangled for recriminations.
a thirsty gadabout. a granular sort of anguish.
a glycerine sheen on the crust.
blues solo of otherworldly creatures dancing on the roof.
a guitar-like incision in the silence.
                                a great night for knick-knackery.
all the stars have come out to bedazzle
                               as we roll back up the hill
none the worst for it to Isabel's uproarious.
we are seasoned to nerve the encounter.
we are quoting Falstaffian lost sagacity.
                        sober as the clouds' full frothiness,
the foot stomping sheep eye us suspiciously.
all the stars glittering their spangles, even the moon even.

Electro-pop lip-synching sonnet

psychedelic pop bands at the pub. Dave on sound
again, so the whole valley is shaking in summer strobe
light with pink purple high notes and dogs are barking
at the wind. so many campers by the river the store
sells out of ice but the bar never runs dry in the picking
season. go bang changa chameleon pnau in the rattle shot
evening with best dance releases won. I'm trying to chill
on a chair in the courtyard, a cat on my knee, ears pricked
to something surprising riding the waves. she doesn't move
though, just settles back to a little mood bending purr.
at least it isn't country she seems to say. the river laughs,
flowers reflect, all the sky diamonds streaming
the last remnants of sun, the neo day trippers testing out
their groove until the black night slips them into silence.

Seasonal

autumn's girth has begun to shed;
bark skin, apples, conkers, little rays
of forgotten light.
days no longer swell and catch
on the fabric of full bloomed worm silk.
rampant vines have choked the mulberry.
leaves turn hot red fuming.
gold leaf gilds the earthling brown.
the festival weaves up the valley
        like smoke in your eyes
        like micro waves
        like salt in your throat.
an aftertaste of music waving in air
dropping little ribbons of blues breath.
as we wander to main stage
there is a shiver of light,
a phantom mist, a fogbow,
between violet and indigo, a blueberry stain.
the dance floor is a crush, a celebration,
an equinoctial wild card.

Bees and wasps and other buzz

*

not caring where I might land on the Schmidt sting pain index
a honey bee darts a level 2 at my face with all the gall
of a trapdoor spider. I bear it with shock and fine words.
I crossed too close to your extinction.

*

considering pest control to shush the jurassic wasp buzz
in my cavities I try to rehouse you with titbits
of antisocial logic.

*

there is a bumble in the garden, a mad migrant here like me.
you are pantomime horse in the gumnuts ignoring committees
and petitions, preferring adventure tourism.

*

bees in my hair.
bees on my washing line.
bees with tears in the succulent clover.
bees in a fish fight with flapping sheets.
bees in my hum and honeycomb bones.

*

an old dovecote is a hiding hive, a waxy memory palace
of whirling honeys. until one day there is a royal death
in the jelly and a black swarm carries a pretender
to a new throne.

*

rehousing buzz friends is a peril.
I won't allow them on my footpaths
or in my mortgaged walls. a man
in a zipped white suit offers tenancy
in gentrified slats with fly screen
out on the dream deck of suburban eyes.

*

and now they are gone. not colony collapse
syndrome or deformed wing virus. just fear dear me.

Night Music

it is 2 a.m. I wake to the screech of a C sharp,
        an anarchic piano nocturne
                echoing from the hall below.

cowed by my fears
        and a metronomic heartbeat
                I grip the banister, descend into dark.

on the old Steinbeck keys a ringtail
        runs the scales in a tinkering din
                terrified by its own new virtuoso.

no pause for bowing it scurries back
        to the imagined safety of the flue,
                the smell of fruit in a bowl causing a diversion.

I switch on the light. he is frozen, caught
        in the act, a plum held in possum paws, he watches it
                bounce, bounce along the table, drop to the floor.

he makes a dash for glass, lays stunned on the floor,
        unconscious briefly in his own reflection.
                he is outside now, looking in,

startled, as if he has only just learnt that
        life is random and ridiculous with
                occasional punctuations of night music.

Loops

from here
the view is sun-splashed
scattershot

bird talk / lifts and drifts / downward slur and warble

a wallaby passes
through an urban garden
moonlit rough edges

scorched earth / pine needles / invasive lavender

peck pecking –
any windswept twig will do
for starlings

light mornings / dark moorings / loops of days on days

Sunset

I watch the clouds
hoist their alabaster sails
into the thick of it;
a night like water.

wind fresh
and full of mosquitoes.

between the lines
red scars and inkings,
a flash of light

as the sun falls
and a new moon scripts the night.

I watch the amaranthine spectrum
into second thoughts–
small moments like this
can question the rural
oxblood of us all.

I pick flowers from shadows.
a cat comes purring back–
a kind of warmth, a ginger lune.
I bin the trash bag as
winter clams shut
the day's unfinished sentence

breath's rhythm
a canopy of old trees
beneath my ribs

Meet me by some river where the egrets are reflecting

balanced on one leg I might fall
in without you.
where the willow bridges.
and the duck's fate is yet
to be chimed. this shady place with
bent light. the leaf's midrib
sharp as spine. mine bent
in tantric speculation.
only the heron's eye is shifting.
it is dewy here with orchids
and harebells floating in October,
aromatics to flavour spring,
chase the native hen away,
its harpy see-saw cutting cry.
meet me by the river's soft reflections.
enough water to drink the light.
enough light to water
the gold swimming by.
we might fall in together.
like love. like drowning.
the egret and me.

Scree Scarp Wind Chill

wind is hurtling
through crevices to trip us from the path
and into another seeing.

before this the path seemed fogged and luteous
the ground scraped boot raw, cobbled;
this muddy path
a jangled
nerve
at the very edge of.

overhangs are for overhanging you say,
reckless as the scrubtit
who builds her nest
in the eagle's flight path.

you slip as you grab a jut of dolerite,
blood axe sharp,
but still you dangle and dare yourself.

I refuse to tremble like the fagus.

the sky drops its back against crags and scree,
looks away from ephemeral things,
will not mourn your skewered bones
fallen into tanglefoot and lanceleaf.

rain, in reproachful mood, is a soaking from the south.
it blocks the view we climbed for,
slaps a spitty warning.

I cling to scrubby walls
of limestone, any rock a refuge.

I am bats' eyes weak.
                    jelly-legged.
                        gimcrack.

I deliberate a life lost in the celery tops.
    your foot misses its footing. pine draws
    blood from your hand, splits, falls
        in a screech and caw of birdsong.

    their agile limbs
the opposite of your, your arms and legs
in a split-second landing clawing at the dirt.

the moss is creeping in
    through
        its long centuries.

    there are pencil pine ghost limbs
scratching the eyes
    out of currawongs.
        these armoured birds.
            their battle shrieks.

    going down again the chill is stinging.

I find myself longing for a walled garden
    with persimmons and lemons,

a goat on the other side of the fence
pruning the overhanging figs.

who am I in this wildness? mascara smudged to black crow eyes. caught up in the insistence of presence but quietly lamenting a broken nail. above me, jagged contours sculpted by wind bluster to organ pipe diaspon. treading the permian sediment unknowing the metallic blue intrusions in the geological sandwich below us. back down again but traversing the violence of pre-cambrian corrugations. the spinifex well spun. gum roots on shallow deposits. bargain boots in the basement squeaking their leaks. my hair wet matted to helmet as we fringe around the edges of damp sclerophyll green. I'm still as dolomite as a snake slides by. in awe of scree scarp wind chill chaos cloud bush sky each-little-leaf-petal-honey-bee. huddled by a rock face. dazed and bedazzled. I'm a tangle of bones waiting for a dash for it. wonder-stricken.

this floor is a ballroom
forest. all flora and
fine fernery. all fungi-like jewellery.
eyes peering from behind
myrtle beech masks.

I am all caught up in
your bouffant coif.

you toss me out of your hair
like a lost yellow-banded dart.

Weather one week

        after dark on Sunday
        wind tucked into branches
        like a lullaby for eggs

the storm we can predict
blows its bluster across strait and sandbar

rainbow picks the teeth of the woodpile

we adhere to the acrylic path
        collagraph
        shellacked and painted –
an unseasonal low moodies the sky

ooh ooh ooh
the notes sax through
moonlight and dew

        moon the setting moon
        slip sliding its light into far ocean

there is a shimmer of oil
on the shoreline's jut of quartz
ship spilt   slick as starfish

The seventh noun from storm

down on the peninsula a storehouse
        and penitentiary formed, performed,
in the particulars of hail and thunder.
        there is a story in the seventh noun from storm.

        fragmented droplets from a faultline
        niggle like a pricked conscience
as a tempest in the harbour soaks the air,
        the sand and any hope of a ghost tour.

        we are told that cell mates slept sitting
for want of space.   in the ground beneath our tent
        rusted iron constrains, warps and needles.
twisted fists knuckle our backs.

        chains once rattled like broken bones
        on ghosts of the island's dead.
now empty bottles rattle in the cooler box.
        thirst and past sins are both things for slaking.

in these waters there is the gut strain
        of struggle, but we just swim and take selfies
in front of ruins. Point Puer has buried its boys.
        the beach is eight out of ten safe now.

        we know they plotted impossible routes
                back to Irish dreams in stolen whale boats,
through rivers, floods and strangled forests.
        we take the short walk back to Stewarts Bay,

tick off the devil park, return to town
in a drowning. at Eaglehawk Neck,
cracks tessellate into pavement,
wave-cut platforms expose the bedrock.

The Pieman

always there are rumours;
the Pieman River named for escapees
consumed in folds of forest, their flesh
degraded in heat and juice for the last man standing.
history folds in detritus, earth to earth. a river guides us.

stained waters are drunk with the taste of tea tree.
a cruiser slides on its glass, pine bark scattering into shards.

ripples carry us backwards to a scrap of shore.
a platypus surfaces for air, its swim a waddle and wave.
we watch an aquatic evasion of hawks and snakes
as it dives back to yabby depths where the marble eyes of fish
check for intruders and felons.

before us: the last of summer, a reckoning,
a sudden downpour, a bridge that has seen better days.

beneath us the alloys are another unearthing. metal
extracted like pulled teeth until work stopped
with a dollar drop in tin, a rise in silicon.
dust to dust. hard labour is commodified and curious.
the river flows with the changes.

an illusion of fresh water and fresh air is here.
drop your feet into distortion, fracture the wavering light.

circles ripple into a page of prose,
echoed above is the choreographed script of peep-wrens.
so easy to be thrown off course by the dissonance
of narrative, until a settlement of sorts unearths
in the nearby fungus whose life is jewel coloured and rare.

behind us: summer's poached heat, simplicity,
the physics of resistance, a bridge that has seen better days.

still the river flows

water falling over rock
small stones silent in the flow
an echidna cautiously wades ashore
        ignores our cumbersome trek
        our junk in the river's veins

petal soft and sore
the frail skin
that binds us

Hand on heart

for John

when they cut your ribs
took out your beating heart
to fix its rhythms,
we held it too; its pulse,
its truth, its full red wine,
its fiery hearth and open fields,
its singing birds and netted gardens,
its spanners, nuts and bolts,
its jazz beats, art strokes,
and secret little chambers,
its brief sliced moment of sterility –
until you woke again, your breath free
from false valves and ticking machinery,
and we could gasp and gasp
and simply hold your hand.

The sky and other mysteries

at 5 you want to know the meaning of it all
and where can I hide but
behind my deficiency.

you ask why the sky is blue. seriously.

the sky is blue because…
some remembered physics about
the scatterings of light waves
and the smallness of blue ones
the colour theories of philosophers…

but why…I distract to passing clouds
looking like marshmallows that day
divert us to stories
and small packets of sometimes foods.

but why, you ask, does the sky
touch the ground but you can't touch it…
but we are touching the air, we're breathing it…
but it isn't blue…

I taught you to read early because I am lazy.
by the time you're 10 I am talking to the hand.
today you teach yourself Brazilian Portuguese for fun
and I am the one asking questions.

if only the sky would stop its blueness
or spread itself conveniently to the ground.

Stroke

held in the palm, it is fragile as the forgotten
scattered legs of a spider, the scald of a cup too hot,
the total of all the sense and movement of a tooling hand.

your caress there, the open impetuous smack,
the feel of silk in the wedding lingerie, the warmth of
hidden places, the wet earth as seedlings are settled into spring,

a baby's head has nestled and imprinted, fingers
sucked by mouth brooders, clothes zipped, washed, pressed,
finely buttoned, dough kneaded into flour, flesh burnt on grills.

the glasswing fingers are hooked now in the confusion
of a question mark. cradled in my hand, as eyes scan and plead
and monitors beep, all that is known is forgotten.

Bookshop

we enter through the door that squeaks on
its old hips, bone to bone.
dried skin of paintwork flakes to dust.
only time can turn paintwork to dust.
only time can shape calf-skinned ghost histories,
pile their cracked vellum spines
and foxed paper into mountain scapes
along passageways.

you have a non-Dewey sorting system.
thick books. thin books. each cover a hook.
stepping over crates on the way to travel,
I'm reminded that Notting Hill was a fiction.
we are not Hugh and Julia. the door sighs.
I gift you WD-40 but you bring it home again
with an old what-the and dead poet poems.

when they interviewed you for the ABC
the door squeaked out in prelude.
they were quick to reference your collection
of bizarre titles, the Harry Potter first editions,
the oldest and the most valuable
but forgot the ephemera boxed in spider silk.

one day we will sell them all and the walls
will breathe out in relief, drop their splintered
shelves into recycle and look out through
freshly spectacled windows. such a retiring
room we will leave for memoir.

Uncharted sailing

hey Eric. you told me once
not to look into the eyes of a stranger's baby
so as not to cause alarm
but to look into the eyes of the mother instead
until the curiosity of the child
offered a pathway to understanding. you taught me the
lesson of thrift in a world that burns its forests
and farms its extremities and chokes
the seas with plastic. you showed me how to gut a fish
(although I prefer to look away until its flesh
is buttered and steaming). you showed me
miniature treasures and sail cloths and patience.
you showed me that pioneers can be fearless
and humble, stoic and tender, adventurous and private.
if you are on that boat, the one you wanted to sail away in,
I know that you are light as wind, strong as stone
and ready to tackle the currents; curious and capable
and steady as you go.

Dear Bruce

I have watched you smile from a peninsula rock
then run through dunes to catch the tide
as a child with the future in your eyes.
I have watched you wind surf along
the tides of ancient beaches catching the sun,
and sail along the horizon framed in light.
I have watched you marry and part, laugh and cry,
rip roar the skies with your humour, then sleep
wherever the moment found you.
I have watched you well then sick again.
I have watched you at all those birthday dinners
with always an outrageously funny tale to tell.
I have watched you juggle life's contradictions
in the depths and the dreams, balance its cruelty
with its beautiful possibilities. I have watched you
set off on adventures, a big-hearted big man
not afraid to express your views, always vulnerable,
always strong. I have watched you serve in an army
uniform and watched you shattered by the secrets
you had to keep. I have watched you care for lost
creatures, fight for the rights of the wounded.
you could whisper and shout and sing.
you could fill a room with your captivating presence
or slip quietly to your hidden places.
you are radiant even in your absence, a last flash
of a dying star that burned with intent and wisdom.

and now I have watched you in a silk lined wooden box,
still as a death we can't yet believe in, always
the first of us to set off on a new adventure. I'm sure
that was a smile on your cold face, a warm goodbye
as we wrestle to understand where the light has gone.

After the funeral

the back roads wind me home again
coiling me in past teatrees, wattle
and ghost gum. the impossibly blue sky
spreads light through every leaf
and branch. I'm held in birdsong –
thrush, kookaburra, magpie, wren;
their little serenade to spring.
each moment the air accepts them,
their tiny hearts declare it.

our place
in the company of mountains
a gentle foothold

A shared path

bare skin
on forest floor,
my scratched soles
the scribble on their bark.

my veins, the veins of myrtle.
        my breath, their breath.
and each twist of limb
        aches like old bone.

the far thicket's
whispered voice
is a shush in the canals
and cochlea of my hearing.

beneath my feet,
        the winding roots
of shared worth, the grip
        and arbour of community.

each curve in the path
is a path already shared,
all bounce and writhe of
animal and tree.

and there is music in it too,
        as we move
to some hidden lifeline's
        rekindled loop and whorl

A lone winter bird

for Marg

I should mention that I know nothing of the
suffering of birds, but here behind the window,
all fluffed up and quivering on a branch,
a story in those wind startled eyes: a waiting.

waiting for the weather to pass perhaps.
wrestling with rain and the full teasing force
of a squall. how hard does that heart beat
beneath the ribs and down?

the blood we know. the aching of joints
and bones. the future planning, one branch
to the next, our version of take-off and
landing. that fixed and anxious look.

she's gone now. flown, we hope, not taken.
into the mystery of sky or to her equivalent
of an evening sip of wine. and not to that other
place; the swollen feathers of sickness.

Two views of the Don

this river has lost itself a bit in tidal pull.
its abandoned banks, scribbled with crab,
are slightly perfumed in resinous air.
it's held together by quick stitch
of darting wren and broad threads
of interweaving limbs. at this time of day
the mud is sleek with remembering,
its clammy hands on exposed
underbelly scratching old wounds.
an old monotreme anxiously seeks its burrow,
scurrying along in silk jacket and slippers.
passing boys throw rocks at it, don't care that
its duckbill is a reminder of impossible things.

a play train on the opposite bank cuts through
in polished red with steam. strokes of scarlet
and yellow abstract a temporary orphism.
electric prisms split de/light en plein air.
someone blows a whistle. (you wonder if that is when
the noose dropped/ if the neck cracked
like the bent ghost gum.) you wonder if cubism is dead,
if placing things in geometrics with light is infinitude
with complications, if juxtapositions are just avoidance.
you wander in decomposition.

Acoustics in forest and air

as the seasons turn more quickly
we reach a gap in the trees,
white noise of motorway
in the distance that wasn't there last year.

my heels dig into bluebell elderberry earth
fruit stained with flute gold,
acorns underfoot watched over
by a stooped oak, held by its mother roots;

wrapped in memory each cell becomes
my cell bone heart shudder.
have you heard the acoustics of trees?
the hiss of moving water to leaves

the whispers shh shushing the bark.
under bower sun stars
each cocked head of bird sussing it out
before bustle and shriek slap of insect

against stark arrow branch, snap
of footsteps axe head quiver of breath
and the leaves shake as the wind hurls through
looking for solitude

in the bee buzz and twitter.
hold me here with fresh forest shiver,
the brush of shimmergreen and fern fruit,
lulled sparrow and squirrel tail,

scatterbrain squeak of fieldmice, coot and snail
in my pulse and skin, my spine resting against
birch, the silver in my hair,
the little words that lose themselves in the

tough bark at the knotted ankles of trees,
their exhale my inhale, all the blood and sap
the sweet smell of blackberry, thorns and dirt
and nettle. fluvial orchestra swimming close by.

and the white noise creeps closer
and the white noise creeps closer and the axe
cuts deeper. the axe cuts deeper. run little deer
before the path exhumes us.

Last catch of the day

a pelican presses the tide, all pride and spitty punctuation
the grab bag at his throat is half full of bream

hunger is a determined master   the fisher fishes on –

see waves crash   as we watch debris fall
oystercatcher's catch   in flash storms
sea cows   cormorant
sea whelks   filigree
seashore   shingle
sea snails   tidal blur and flotsam

see the wave   billow   from rough waters
fall in a crash   & bang   and lose its white crown
as it swallows   crabs   & starfish

estuary's mouth   a dull line   bobs for flathead
as the sun dips   a lone boat   tilts the horizon
a silvery tail   flicks   into leathery oblivion
reluctant moon   ascending   is half dreaming

Sometimes the sun

S
S
S
S
S
ome
times the sun
just pops its globe.
I wait there in broken grass
in the shard light between shadows,
half lit but not dim & above me in the plum
tree a ringtail holds its fruit as you hold a book of
poems, just as mindfully. dark juice is sucked from its casing.

the air is
in splinters. we're held
here
& it is
beautiful.
but it still can't explain

why when
the light
slips I see
more.

Ghosts

all those little bones in red clay
as worn as the heart-free stones.   by the river,
a coil of spine, its head missing but entrails
reddening the earth it moved through.   a shard of bright
sunlight catches your eye.
you pick up a stick and gently probe its mysteries
stirring for ghosts.   they are everywhere.

> from my window, a tree-lined paddock,
> gum trees, acacia yellow, winter intruded berries,
> clapping of leaves, discarded feather of a wren
> missing its bony frame but hovering still.

those hands that formed me transformed to air now.
silence is weightless.   light abandoned
as the old spaces cancel their language.

here or there impossible moving ghosts
        shimmering their twitched nerves.

Riffle and flux

it was a last minute
decision
turn left not right
follow the river's course
and never curse its
ambivalence
stale red geraniums
have morphed
into fagus
gold
baby myrtle scrapes
our boots
the path slides
into sand and stone
a letting go
like waters rush
over rocks to calmly
glaze
the lower flats
with a lazy balm
of tea tree leaves
the flow never stops
to edify us
we reflect
as we kneel
to drink safe
palmfuls here
and there
the pademelon hides

Acknowledgements

The following poems have been previously published:
'a baby wren' and 'our place' in *Haiku Wales*
'Flood proof' in *Australian Poetry* anthology
and *Wild* anthology, Ginninderra Press
'Monofilament is best' in Australian Poetry online 'poem of the week' series, winning 'poem of the year'
'6 equal pieces' and 'Minor domestic emergencies' in
Cordite Poetry Review
'beneath the colour purple' and 'streak of lightning' in
One hundred gourds
'The poppy picker' in *Australian Poetry Journal*
'Sudden shower over Ulverstone bridge' and 'Jury duty' in
Regime magazine
'Minor domestic emergencies' in *Australian Poetry* anthology
'A poem with needles in it' in *I protest* anthology,
Ginninderra Press
'Sunset' in *Crow*, Ginninderra Press
'The sky and other mysteries' and 'Night Music' in
Rabbit Journal RMIT
'Stroke' in *Australian Poetry Sotto* journal
'Swimming above the belly of the earth' in
Australian Poetry anthology

My sincere and continuing gratitude
to all the editors and publishers.

My sincere thanks to Stephen Matthews at Ginninderra Press for his professionalism, support and opportunity.
And my heartfelt thanks to writing companions and friends Kristen Lang and Kim Nielsen-Creeley for encouragment, especially to Kristen, for insightful input during the editing of this collection.

With love, I would also like to express gratitude to my daughter, Sophie Jermy, for her cover design, and to Pete and Sophie for all the precious moments we share.

www.ingramcontent.com/pod-product-compliance
Lightning Source LLC
Chambersburg PA
CBHW050302120526
44590CB00016B/2453
* 9 7 8 1 7 6 1 0 9 4 0 6 4 *